UNITED NATIONS

AGENDA 21:

"THE

BIG

LIE"

By: Dennis Andrew Ball

author, THE BALL DOCTRINE:

"Creating Peace & Prosperity In Every Nation!"

Copyright © 2019 Dennis Andrew Ball

ISBN 13: 9781729786420
10:1729786421

DEDICATION

"THIS BOOK IS DEDICATED TO AMERICANS

WHO SACRIFICE EVERYDAY TO PRESERVE

PROTECT & DEFEND OUR LIBERTY &

FREEDOM FOR OUR CHILDREN&

GENERATIONS TO COME!

NOW THE TIME HAS COME FOR A NEW

GENERATION OF AMERICANS TO TAKE THE

REIGNS OF STATE & MAKE THEM WORK AS

THEIR OWN IN THE BEST INTERSTS OF THE

PEOPLE, THEIR CHILDREN, THEIR FAMILIES

AND GENERATIONS TO COME!

TABLE OF CONTENTS

Dedication

Acknowledgment

Authors' Foreword

____

ACKNOWLEDGMENT

To The COURAGE of UN Secretary General Dag Hammarskjold Demonstrated At A Time Of Great Danger To Our Nation During Uncertain Times In American & World History.

Author's Foreword

I am reminded by history past the history of the United States would not be complete if it were not for those gallant men and women who in the face of danger, proceeded to do something Special about it! America's very existence is tied to her economic health which requires this generation understand & participate that being a citizen is more than thinking about it but knowing what to do about it that "frees" oneself to become the solution for our children & generations to come.

UNITED NATIONS
AGENDA 21: "THE BIG LIE!"

Since the death of President Kennedy, events in America and the World have continued to show all of us how vulnerable our economic system is to currency manipulation and deficit spending by governments and the Congress of these United States, the result being a bloated deficit with borrowing and spending unaccountable to The Citizenry & States of these United States; including fiscal policies, laws and acts contrary to The BEST INTERESTS of ALL Americans. This is the ROOT of the social problems created within and by American society, fueled by OPPORTUNISTS, CARPETBAGGERS, USERS, MISUSERS & ABUSERS OF THE PEOPLE TO VOMENT DIVISION & CLASS WARFARE!

6

1. INTRODUCTION.

The *history of America* would not be complete if it were not for the men and women who sacrificed so much of themselves for a new nation and its children. Of course, much can be said of those who plotted against them and used them to profit at their expense. For those they must answer for us we must correct their mistakes for our children and generations to come. This then becomes the back ground and back drop of *ENEMIES OF THE CONSTITUTION: "The Plot To Take Down America!"*

"You cannot help the poor by destroying the Rich." "You cannot keep out of trouble by spending more than you earn." "You cannot lift the wage earner by pulling down the wage payer" – Abraham Lincoln

---

"I have always been afraid of banks."

"One man with courage makes a majority" "It is to be regretted that the rich and powerful too often bend the acts of government to their own selfish purposes." "Take time to deliberate but when the time for action arrives, stop thinking and go in." – *Andrew Jackson*

Let it be said, that America's finest hours are yet to come because the Children Of America can make a contribution to not only our Nation but also the World!

We are the product of generations past, present and future with the belief that our rights come from God; NOT THE STATE at a great cost to those who fought and died for them! That was the Social Contract created in 1781 at Yorktown-Gloucester Bay, Virginia.

The monuments laid at the reefs of those so honored are a testament to the sacrifice of so many for the hope that their sacrifice would *bear.* A proud nation was born and with it the

8

greatest nation on earth in the history of man, *"AMERICA!"*

THE NATIONAL BACKGROUND
Early History

What was assumed by those in power was taken for granted by those struggling to live out their dreams. *AMERICA* was a land of opportunity because it's people made it their priority to continue living out their dreams for a better life for themselves and those for their children.

Colonial America grew at an astounding rate by the span of time from the founding of the Republic at Jamestown, Virginia 1607 until the last entry known as Georgia Colony 1732.

Of course, many events in between the time of founding and establishing Colonial life dominated the culture legally and politically; particularly making it possible for 2.5 million people to realize their value because the Bible

9

was read in the home, the schools and the Supreme Court! Ethics & Morales were also taught in the home practicing honesty and good business including honest services. The attitudes within the culture was fairness as the colonies grew in population and farming. As a result, the *Great Migration* ensued so that by the beginning of the War For Independence, *AMERICA* had enough population to fight England for it. And so we did on July 4, 1776 by way of the Declaration Of Independence, Congress, Philadelphia, Pennsylvania.

Now comes ENEMIES OF THE CONSTITUTION redefining the current rules based on the *16th Amendment to the Constitution of these United States.* What does it say and what does it mean?

"*CONGRESS,* shall have power to lay & collect taxes on incomes without regard to any census or enumeration. There was an income tax *prior* to this

10

Amendment & it was in effect during Civil War." Ratified February 3, 1913

So, what we have here is a system of taxation based on representation of enumeration of census as to the number of folks occupy individual states. However, this Amendment did away with the census enumeration and went to a direct tax on income which now includes the Standard Deduction and deductions based on losses and gains. Could it be those with the most to lose tie themselves up with the government for as long as necessary to keep themselves from being penalized for surreptitious acts they commit during the period of doing their business? Therefore, no "free" lunch just tax.

That is my point, unlike the history of *.Early America* when life and government was much simpler and much smaller than now, we Americans did not have to deal with so

11

much regulation and taxation without representation. Executive session was the oddity not common practice as is *today.*

And So, since President William Howard Taft, a man who held Office as both President and later as Chief Justice, history records his participation in the events that mark 1913 as a Turning point in American history.

Events do have a way of marking themselves to follow the outcome of what creates tremendous conflicts and tragedy in the lives of our Citizens and the outcome for our Children.

It is within this context that government *Of, By & For The People* will survive and thrive in this the twenty-first century and beyond. We will need to understand how we got here and what we must do to preserve, protect & defend our liberty & freedom.

2.SUSTAINABLE DEVELOPMENT

ICLEI – International Council For Local
Environmental Initiatives

The man that betrayed America and made
us into a debtor nation! Woodrow Wilson,
United States President signed into law
Federal Reserve Act, December 23, 1913.

He was also the President that led the
United States into World War 1 at the behest
of the International Banking Cartel who
financed both World Wars and have ever

since! How convenient!

This is what Presidents' Washington, Lincoln and Jackson warned Americans not to let government become BIG Government at the expense of the Common man. They knew our economic health depended upon the strength of a strong dollar able to compete in the Global Marketplace unimpeded by fraud and schemes supporting family values.

In Europe, the same holds true especially in the United Kingdom. Both The House Of Lords & The House Of Commons take their marching orders from the Queen of England closely administered by the Central Bank Of England located in London as a City State.

That is how the International Monetary Fund & World Bank became the Central Banks of Europe by following policy from the Crown. All the other countries followed its lead and created what today is the European Union which ironically recently the UK

14

withdrew by a vote of the people. To many Brits, especially the Ruling Class, the EU has become an albatross around their necks by it's economic and political policies and interests.

The Federal Reserve Act of 1913 set the stage for economic chaos not only for America but the entire World! Manipulation of currency laws in every country based on Central Bank policy has put the Bankers in control of the World; not THE PEOPLE!

There is a complete disconnect between what is *fair* and what is *just!* By making nations debtors to the Banks, the children & families suffer for lack of "equitable advantage". Laws that govern borrowing and spending create debt by which those in control benefit handsomely at the debtors expense which in many cases are families. More will be written about this subject as I lay out a plan to restore the family both economically and emotionally in their BEST INTERESTS for generations to come.

The Act cemented in the minds of many Banks to administer the flow of currency and capital to their members. But again, the price was a Surrender of economic sovereignty to the banks which is the root of the problem in the World. "He that controls the Gold controls the Nation State", said Lord Cromwell. The *history* of the corruption does not stop there.

1913 was an interesting year for America not only for the signing by President Wilson but the ratification of the 16th Amendment by The State Of Wyoming providing ¾ majority of states necessary to amend the Constitution.

The first IRS 1040 also rolled out to finance Wars as it continues today. The Banker's Cartel begins to roll since their secret meeting 1910 on the Resort Jekyl Island, GA.

THE ENEMIE'S LIST GROWS!

How the 'Nation State' has survived is a testament to Providence in spite of years of abuse by forces foreign to the sacrifice & commitment of its Citizens.

Who are the "Enemies Of The Constitution?" They are many and long. Once you study the history of America Since Abraham Lincoln, you realize Americans have been set-up for failure by an elitist class of wealth driven thugs.

Their corruption has no limits, no bounds. conspiring together in 1910 on Jekyl Island, Georgia the bankers with the support of those in Congress devised a scheme by which the American people were deceived by stalking it's members with promises of better government financed by income taxes ruled unconstitutional in 1895 by the United States Supreme Court.

17

Since then with events to come, the country and our culture have been vulnerable to attack by different groups who's agenda to kill the Goose that lays the golden eggs.

We must fight back by showing our resolve that economic freedom is synonymous with economic liberty; without both, we are Subjects of the State and rendered 'useful idiots', contrary to the to the Bill Of Rights and Constitution of these United States, in effect, a Feudal System.

The enemies list covers a lot of sins that have their origins in the pockets of the American people. With the income tax being established to pay interest on debt by Treasury, the stage was set to tax our wages and our profits in spite the Supreme Court said it unconstitutional on income from

18

wages. That is why the Fair Tax eliminates the income tax and replaces it with tax on spending. Read THE FAIR DEAL for more.

But in a broader sense the enemies list comprises those who have an aversion of subverting the Constitution designed to protect the American people from abusive government from within the government.

The other side are those forces outside the government wishing to take down the Republic by all means possible. These players are rooted in their own 'ism' "foreign" to our culture and work ethic of production and equity. Those groups must be exposed replaced by those who believe in Fairness & Rule of Law.

The policing mechanism on the Republic must come by The People themselves by becoming Citizen Candidates educated in that which works versus Generalities &

Vagaries.

For this, I have authored several titles to fill the void. I will continue to speak about the plot to take down America witnessed best by those that knew & did something about it during their time. It is our duty to continue their legacy to fight & succeed against all threats both foreign & domestic including the three branches of the Federal government and those in State & Local government.

SUSTAINABLE DEVELOPMENT is a catch word created to instill stability into Communities of class mobility. The problem is finding people qualified to do the jobs that industry requires to invest themselves within their community.

Skilled labor is synonymous building economic security within family unity. I find this thought sorrowfully lacking in the political and economic dialogue of every nation. AGENDA 21 makes everyone equal in an unequal world; not because people are stupid but because they are not challenged to think outside conventional thinking.

Free enterprise capitalism has always been the hallmark and path building success.

INTERNATIONAL COUNCIL FOR LOCAL ENVIROMENTAL INITIATIVES -ICLEI

Summed up this organization tied to the United Nations intrudes itself into the affairs of local governments opposed to ideas that are independent and sovereign to their own.

Originally, the Charter of the UN was designed to instill amongst nations the principles of human rights guiding the nations to independence and sovereignty. Today, that does not exist and threatens the security of nations within their Charter.

THE BALL DOCTRINE can and will change the discussion from dependence on the State to independence for The People.

Families, children generations to come are at stake. National Sovereignty is the issue that unites local governments working in **concert with the** Best Interests of The People.

Without this in play, a sure disaster is being created for all People outside this Scam of One World Government.

3. PRESIDENT KENNEDY.

1919-1963

"The High Office Of The President Has Been Used To Foment A Plot To Destroy The Americans' Freedom & Before I Leave Office I Must Inform The Citizens Of This Plight".

President John Fitzgerald Kennedy, Columbia University November. 12, 1963.

What the President alluded to was the pernicious attitude upon the nation by the Cartel of International Bankers President Woodrow Wilson had signed into law a day prior to Christmas Eve December 23, 1913.

The Federal Reserve Act was a continuation of the financial abuse created upon the nation prior to its signing, in 1791 & 1816. Only Old Hickory shut down the Bank Of The United States in 1836 paying off the Federal Debt of $7,000,000.00 with The Federal Treasury. It still stands today.

Because of what the Banking Cartel had done to the nation, President Kennedy was intent in undoing. Because the Federal Reserve Bank is a Central Bank its Charter exempted it from accountable oversight to any government entity. Its powers had to be reigned in.

John Kennedy made it his business to do just that by signing E.O. 11110 effectively transferring control of the Bank out of their hands to the United States Treasury. This in turn had the chilling effect of neutralizing the Bank's Charter putting it out of business. The Gold Standard still was backing US Dollar currency for The People.

Signed June 4, 1963, the Order provided for the printing of both Silver Certificates & United States Notes exempting the words Federal Reserve Note. Both bills showed their authenticity to the United States Treasury and were circulated prior to and shortly after President Kennedy's death November 22, 1963. That Order has never been rescinded but ignored by every President since Kennedy. The National debt does not belong to the American People but to the private banking cartel known as the Federal Reserve Bank Of NY & its Branches!

Interest was exempt from the debt!

**** (for educational Art display only)

RS - ($2.00 United States Note Circa 1963)

RS - ($5.00 United States Note Circa 1963)

****(for   educational   Art   display   only)

4. UNITED NATIONS -ICLEI

International Council Of Local
Environmental Initiatives

1947 was a turning point for the World and how the future of it would turn.

The United Nations was born as an answer to Woodrow Wilson's LEAGUE OF NATIONS that got abandoned by nations concerned with their own sovereignty.

President Franklin Roosevelt envisioned a Council of Nations committed to arbitrating conflicts that could threaten the security of nations. However, what wasn't considered is the potential of those same nations creating Global instability within the Body Politic.

Official Title: an alternative solution -

AS introduced – To promote freedom, fairness, & economic opportunity by repealing The Income Tax & other taxes, abolishing the Internal Revenue Service; enacting a National

27

Sales Tax to be administered primarily by the States.

Under the bill, the States have the responsibility for collecting & remitting the sales tax to the United States Treasury. Tax Revenues are to allocate amongst 5 groups. They are:

1. General Revenue Funds.

2. Old-age & Survivors Insurance Trust Fund.

3. Disability Insurance Trust Fund.

4. Hospital Insurance Trust Fund.

5. Federal Supplementary Medical Insurance Trust Fund.

NO FUNDING is authorized for the operations of Internal Revenue Service after Fiscal Year [FY2021].

The Bill terminates the national sales tax if the Sixteenth Amendment to the Constitution (authorizing an income tax) is not repealed within seven years after the enactment of this bill.

28

United States Senate Version:

S. 18 - Introduced Senator Jerry Moran, [R-KS] 1/3/2017. The Senate version is similar to that of the House but for a few additions and subtractions including a monthly sales tax rebate based on size of family and poverty guidelines. Both bills still have a lot of work to do upon which a Balance Budget Amendment to the Constitution is also necessary to keep government from overspending by bad policy that encourages it including a tax rate of 23% the first year which is much too high.

What is necessary is for the States to take back responsibility to tell the Federal Government how much money they are to fund essential services and DOD. The purpose of government is to protect its Citizens from threats to their lives, property money and Bill Of Rights; NOT TO GROW AN OUT OF CONTROL GOVERNMENT AT THE EXPENSE OF ITS CITIZENS.

In my book "BALLONOMIC$: "Lifting America & The World Out Of Poverty From The Bottom Up!", I address the issues of Entrepreneurship skilled labor education; attracting industry to create a "living wage".

THE CHANGING ROLES OF THE UN

5. OPEN BORDERS

The Federal Government is undisciplined by design the case for a balanced budget and with it a Balanced Budget Amendment.

The case can also be made that unfunded mandates it creates causes harm to the States by depleting their resources for the citizens in their State. Add these enemies to the list.

SOPHISTRY has literally changed the Mission & Purpose of Federal government to one of consumption & waste of Taxpayer dollars.

Entitlements, Earmarks, Pork, Mandates, Gerrymandering and getting re-elected with few term limits have caused a burgeoning national debt and crisis of confidence in our nation's economy.

How much more can the nation endure

until real change addresses the real problems of Income Inequality? Only time will tell, but in this author's humble opinion, it needs to start NOW!

The budget of the United States has always been a hot button issue because of the demands of government on The People.

One can compare their own experience to everyday life of demands placed on our time and resources. So it is with problems created by government and an out-of-control undisciplined spending that causes harm to our nation and our lives.

To correct that requires more than wishful thinking. We must have a plan and make it a part of our national dialogue and life. "WE CAN!""WE WILL!" should be a slogan echoed in the Halls of Congress.

Our children will thank us for making it and them our priority to secure their futures and those to come.

Replacing the 16th Amendment with a Balance Budget Amendment makes sense. Bridling the Federal Budget from politicians who use their position to buy votes with tax payer dollars in the form of Pork, Earmarks Mandates, Entitlements, Sophistry is wrong!

How many school lunch programs for little kids are we depriving by masking our true intentions in ways that hurt our nation and our Children?

On the streets of Washington D.C. I witnessed in 2012 homeless people and families sleeping on the streets and sides of buildings for not enough food to eat or a place to sleep. In a country as rich as

these United States, I saw what poverty does
to people and the aftermath of hopelessness
makes. Skilled Labor prevents that social
experience of homelessness. Making life
affordable is the challenge we face and it
starts with the budget economy that works
for all Americans and their families. From
there, Citizenship becomes the responsibility
of us all to see our children are educated
and our community productive. Skilled labor
solves a multitude of problems politicians
create and ignore at the people's expense.

A Balanced Budget amendment will keep
Federal departments from overspending and
gaming the system for more resources the
next fiscal year. With the States processing
the tax on consumption, they will be in the
position to take control of the purse to

34

empower them to control the size and depth of the Federal government because controls on spending and borrowing do not exist. It is within their discretion based on revenues collected at the State level to fund having the effect of limiting the size of government and its wasteful spending practices on non-essential services & programs based on the taxes in their control.

Years of financial and economic abuse by lawmakers, educators, attorneys whose behavior is negative toward society & the traditional family, have caused all of us a great deal of anxiety and trepidation.

It is in this context that the enemies of the Constitution are many of which their numbers are legion by which to explore.

Open borders means illegal immigration

and the violation of national sovereignty.

The UN Charter was never intended to become a wedge to divide nations within. It is common knowledge that their charter was designed to support the mediation of conflicts; not create them.

Open borders is a recipe for disaster and threatens national sovereignty of nations allowing numbers of people coming into a country. The United Nations has a problem with national sovereignty. This is no good.

New World Order Organizational Chart

Illuminati Royal Bloodlines

Rothschild
Astor • Bundy
Collins • DuPont • Freeman
Kennedy • Li • Onassi • Rockefeller • Disney
Russell • Van Duyn • Merovingian • Reynolds

Foundation nations of the New World Order

America   England   Israel   Australia   China

Financial Groups	Research Institutions	Secret Societies
IMF	Institute For Policy Studies	P2/Opus Dei
World Bank	Stanford Research Institute	Rosicrucions
Central Banks	Brookings Institute	Freemasonry
Federal Reserve	Tavistock Institute	Skull & Bones
Bank of-	Committee of 300	Bohemian Club
International Settlement	Aspen Institute	The Knights of Malta
	Jason Society	

Political	Intelligence	Religious	Educational
Council on Foreign Relations	MI-5	World Parliment of Religions	UNESCO
Trilateral Commission	CIA	National Council of Churches	Lucis Trust
Governmental Leaders	NSA/FBI	World Council of Churches	World Union
U.S. Supreme Court &	KGB	Christian Fundimentalists	World Goodwill
Electorial College	Interpol	Temple of Understanding	Esalen Institute
NATO • EU • EEC	MOSSAD	Universalist Churches	Planetary Congress
United Nations	Drug Cartels	New Age Cults	Media Establishment
Bilderbergers	Homeland Security	Vatican/Jesuits	World Federalist Assc.
Club of Rome	Military Intelligence	Satanists	World Constitution Assc.

Corporations, Multinationals and Banks
Supporting the New World Order Agenda

Bechtel • Carlyle Group • TRW • Raytheon • Rand • WalMart • Texas Utilities
Atlantic Richfield-Arco • Exxon-Esso-Mobil • Texaco • Shell Oil • Tenneco • Corning
Dow Jones • MBNA Citigroup • Chase Manhattan • Bank America • Bankers Trust
Glaxo SmithKline • Archer Daniels Midland • Chemical Banking • Schering Plough
Goldman Sachs • American Express • AT&T • Philip Morris • Boeing • Amtrak
Northwest Airlines • American Airlines Ford Motors • Chrysler • General Motors
Deere • Nabisco • Coca Cola PepsiCo • Anheuser Busch • McDonalds • Burger King
Altria (Philip Morris/Kraft) • Blackstone Group Chevron-Texaco (Caltex) • BP-Amoco
GE • Enron • Daimler/Chrysler • Unisys • ITT • Xerox • Intel • IBM • Motorola
Dell • Levi Strauss • Motorola • Johnson & Johnson • Bristol Myers • Squibb
Eli Lily • Pfizer • Kissinger Assoc. • Amway • Monsanto/Solutia • Dow Chemical
News Corp Limited Inc • Time Warner/AOL • Disney • CBS • NBC • ABC • PBS AP
CNN • Reuters • Washington Times • Children's TV Workshop • U.S. News & W.R.
New York Times • Time, Inc. • Newsweek • Washington Post • Wall Street Journal

6. IMMINENT DOMAIN.

"Our Problems As A Nation Is An
Electorate Given To Fraud & Schemes"

Because NO provision was written into
The United States Constitution regulating
Borrowing or spending by the Congress of
these United States, there exists and has for
years, a problem regulating the National
Debt beginning in 1913 continuing until
now.

That problem is DEFICIT SPENDING.
borrowing and paying Interest on the Debt
with taxpayer dollars out of the Federal
Treasury. This is what George Washington
warned America at its founding and to keep
America "Free" from its burden as if foreign
Army's had absconded with government

property without ever firing a shot!

In our history, the problem has grown to become UNACCOUNTABLE DEFICIT BORROWING & SPENDING making it IMPOSSIBLE for the Federal Government to police itself without shutting it down.;

Our history also shows that since 1913, *America* has failed to put in place safeguards to prevent this unaccountable cycle to come to an END!. WE THE PEOPLE, demand that this government stop it's endless cycle for the good of our Country, our Children and Generations to come!

The Ruling Banking Families in the Federal Reserve Central Bank know exactly the burden they have created by design upon the American people & their children. They know the bigger the debt on the nation the

greater their profits from the DEFICIT.
They are not about to reduce it because
they know they don't have too. But that
does not release them from the liability
of their FRAUD on the nation. Specifically,
Executive Order 11110 signed June 4,
1963 by then President John Fitzgerald
Kennedy transferring control of America's
monetary system to the United States
Treasury.

We can see that in June 1963, America
Borrowed $305,859,632,996.41 backed by
Gold & Silver.   Today, the debt has grown
and keeps growing to unacceptable limits
all to make the Bankers more money on
interest charged on THEIR DEBT.

-Here's The Evidence-

From 1963 to 1999 The National debt climbed from $305,000,000,000.00 billions to over $5,000,000,000,000.00 trillions.in a matter of 36 years. Now it is approaching $21,000,000,000,000,.00 with trillions in Unfunded mandates stuck to the States.

The Cartel has made its business to loan the Federal Government any amount of *fiat* currency it requires as long as it pays the interest on the debt. They have also made it their business to cause harm to Citizens by causing the government to collect taxes to pay them. The debt however, cannot be paid *but it can be forgiven.*

How? Because it is backed by nothing! The same people who formed the Cartel sold the Country that the Banks would take care

41

of the financial needs of the nation so long as the nation paid them interest on the debt. The Federal Reserve System is neither Federal nor a Reserve of Currency nor a System. It is in effect a Banker's Cartel who lends *fiat currency with no value for interest payments to the members of the Cartel every month administered by the IRS & Treasury.*

This relationship was designed by the Scientists of the Federal Reserve System. They knew exactly what they should do to make the "System" work for them opposite the American Taxpayer.

In effect, it is a corrupt institution that Funds the International Monetary Fund & The World Bank.

There is absolutely no evidence that Executive Order 11110 signed June 4, 1963 has been rescinded or the wording that nullified it despite other President's issues.

We are left that since every President since Lyndon Johnson, has ignored it that perhaps fearful that if they were to follow its directive, they too might be killed. Both Lincoln and Kennedy believed the *Nation* should issue and regulate its own currency, not a foreign bank masquerading around as a Federal entity but a private banking cartel.

The nation had seen this before during the presidency of Andrew Jackson (1829-1837).

 THE BANK OF THE UNITED STATES was shut down by Jackson but an attempt was made on his life. Jackson, founder of the Democratic Party surmised as warned by

George Washington that the currency of the nation was sovereign to the United States Treasury and should stay in its control both in the manufacturing and minting of printed and coined currency.

The inflation non-backed currency wars on the dollar devaluing the dollars' worth in terms of purchasing power and payment of debt release. Diluting the economy with unbacked green backs is a recipe for more inflation and higher prices.

Backed securities with Gold or Silver makes for a much more stable economy disallowing the government from over spending and causing families harm by a reckless and selfish policy of greed.

REAL CAPITALISM will cause the Federal government to shrink because it will no longer be able to control a rogue policy of self enrichment at the expense of the taxpayers and their families. The Federal government will have to learn to live within its means like Citizens must live within a budget. The Charter Bank will replace the Central Bank aka Federal Reserve System.

The boom and bust cycles in the *history* of the nation is over. Economic prosperity for America will be measured in real dollars backed by Gold or Silver instead of nothing!

The national debt will be gone and the dawning of a new era in funding will begin! War bonds, Saving Bonds, Treasury Bills all have their place raising money for worthy Causes and Investments for the The People!

Imminent Domain is the taking by govt. your money, property, family & freedom!

7. GLOBAL COMPACT MIGRATION

SUPPOSEDLY THE COMPACT FAILS
TO ENCOURAGE MIGRATION NOR
DISCOURAGE IT. IT IS WHAT THE
STATES DETERMINE IT TO MEAN.
It says: "The Global Compact reaffirms the
Sovereign right of States to determine their
National migration policy & prerogative to
Govern migration within their jurisdiction,
in conformity with international law. Within
their sovereign jurisdiction, States may
distinguish between regular and irregular

migration status, including as they determine their legislative and policy measures for the implementation of the Global Compact, taking into account different national realities, policies, priorities & requirements for entry, residence and work, in accordance with international law."

The conference was held at Marrakech, Morocco, December 10th & 11th, 2018 allowing each nation to present their positions whether good or bad.

Being non-binding, the nations could opt-out or in the alternative recognize the consequences of illegal immigration on their countries.

A crisis is created amongst the nation's the United Nations has contributed. Their

47

attitudes and policies of Global domination

by bringing in One World Government is here. It is our duty as citizens everywhere to stop and block their policies that destroy national borders and sovereign territories.

This is the single most intrinsic problem within Border States and with it penalties that follow on The People. Simply put, nations are not suppose to absorb to support migrant nations. Nations are suppose to support themselves, their families and their children.

Anything less is an abrogation of their Duty to their nation's citizens and their National Security.

The threat of Chain Migration using New born children fleeing for political

48

asylum makes the case for a strong border WALL be erected to counter the growing threats of political ideologies and diseases coming to the borders of these United States. To undermine our sovereignty and security by advocating migration a human right. That is a position unacceptable to many nations upon which backlash to it is ongoing.

One World Government must have a common theme amongst nations to bind them together. Environment, Immigration, Healthcare Terrorism are major topics defining the conversation.

With sponsorship coming from the UN, Nations are encouraged to sign surrendering their sovereignty to a World Body.

One World Government New World Order is just around the corner unless We

49

The People take back that which is lost by those against LIBERTY AND FREEDOM.

NEGATIVE ASPECTS THE GC DOCUMENT DOES NOT ADDRESS:

The Welfare State is thriving by this document because of free stuff. Migrants v. Refugees are different. One is illegal; the other is legal if truthful.

Power and control to support the New World Order based on population control. Import migrants to make up the low level of births. The tax payers must fund all of this Migration. Who says? The UN! Get the Nations out of the United Nations. It is a slithering sloth to con The People to believe lies and deception.

Welfare is not free. Muslims gravitate to free stuff. Cut them off, they will leave.

Our history as a nation must return to a *Nation* of laws enforced by its Citizens upon unelected bureaucrats who use their agency to personally profit at taxpayer expense. We cannot continue to allow their conduct to impact our lives or that of our families. The time has come to act and fulfill President Kennedy's vision for America & the World!

America's destiny demands her people do for her children that which requires their economic and political security, benefit and welfare for now and generations to come.

To do that means being educated in the misconduct of this government creating a new model by which its Citizens function.

Unlike the Federal Reserve ACT, THE FAIR DEAL does not require an Amendment to the Constitution to make

51

it work. It is suggested and recommended for a Balance Budget Amendment replace it to keep the government's budget in check with its income.

Since 1913, the Federal government is dependent on tax and spend policies that cause harm to our children and families.

Inflation on prices of goods and services can be directly attributed to the number of non-backed currency dollars floating from the Federal Reserve Bank. Whether its an entry on their computers, the debt continues to grow which the cartel wants to realize the income on interest that debt generates to it.

Why this is allowed to continue should be of great concern to The People of the United States. Until this is changed and a new model appears, *America* will continue to be held hostage to the bankers and their families.

In addition, the *National Debt* as a Product of the Gross National Product (GDP) is comprised of Public, Foreign Countries, and Americans. But the Federal Reserve Banks lend to the Federal government and that debt should go away. That would reduce the National Debt by 70% with the reset owed to trusts and countries.

That would greatly reduce the stress created on the taxpayers to support the debt. In effect it would relieve the burden on the people to keep more of their hard earned dollars in their pockets thereby increasing their ability to save and build an equity for themselves and their families.

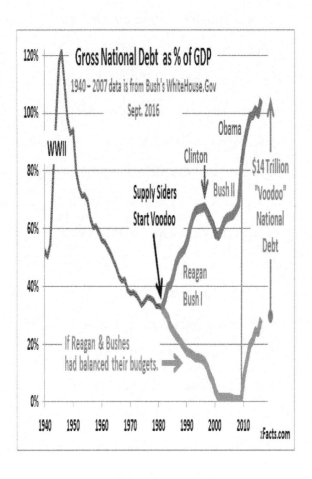

We can see from the graph how the debt is allocated and what needs to be done to rein it back. Some called it from the harm some call "Voodoo Economics" by which a cut in taxes is supposed to create a surplus by increased revenues.

A Fair Tax eliminates that problem and because revenues are based on spending and a balanced budget. That's how you keep this government solvent & its tax paying citizens able to support themselves, their families and their communities including building liquidity and equity in their bank accounts.

The enemies list continues to grow and with it an appreciation of the sacrifices made by the Citizenry of these United States. Can we do any less for our children & others?

8. DEPOPULATION

In 1992, inventory & control plan ALL 179 nations agenda for the 21st Century.

Communitarism should be balanced against the rights of the community. Regionalization is stepping stones to Globalization is the standardization of ALL Systems.

Total control central government One World Government. Public private partnerships. Economy, ecology, social equity. THE BIG LIE! Impoverishing huge portions of the population & bringing down the developed nations.

A Corporatocracy being developed a Totalitarian State right now all over the World. Their goal to reduce the population.

Global, regional, neighborhoods describes AGENDA 21. Land control for Regionalization eliminates representative government. Movement of people is unfathomable to stack & pack the rural areas into the cities. The goal to control & restrict the free movement of populations for their control. It equates to a concentration camp. Surveillance and control moving people off their lands to the will of the State!

THE GENOCIDE TREATY:

A treaty ratified 1988 by United States Senate signed by President Ronald Reagan. Power & Control by government common to all.

Reagan said the problem with government

is that they know so much that they put "common sense" on trial. The treaty in fact created a conundrum that still exists even as far as today where countries may be unaccountable for what individuals do within them. Here is the Treaty Contents:

ITS CONTENTS ARE UNINTELLIGIBLE. REAGAN SIGNED A TREATY THAT GAVE NATIONS PRACTICING THE PRACTICE OF GENOCIDE ON THEIR CITIZENS CART-BLANCHE BY THEIR VERY PARTICIPATION. THAT WAS NOT THE INTENT OF THE ORIGINAL TREATY AUTHORED BY THE U.N. IN 1946 AT THE END OF WORLD WAR II.

THIS IS A SERIOUS BREACH OF U.S.

FOREIGN POLICY THAT MUST BE
CORRECTED IN THE EYES OF THE
CONSTITUTION & PUNISHMENTS.

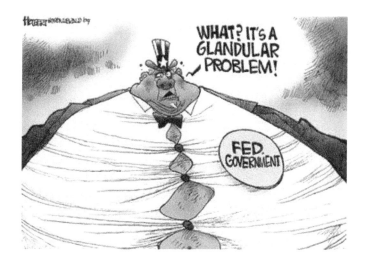

Where Was Common Sense by signing this treaty failing to hold nations accountable?

<u>FREE SPACE</u>

9. THE BALL DOCTRINE:
"The Rise & Fall of Modern Empires"

As though time and distance could be seen into a looking glass what is to come, history shows us what has happened to nations when the laws of economic$ are violated by those in authority.

No doubt, the nations of the World still have much to learn from the mistakes of previous generations culminating in their demise. The graph below illustrates nations' who in fact make those mistakes.

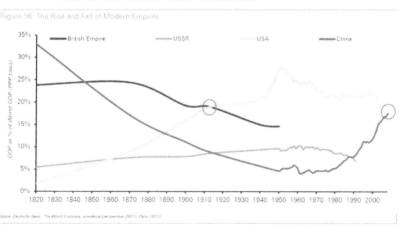

Figure 96 The Rise and Fall of Modern Empires

61

It would appear to this author that for years the economic policies that created mass chaos within market conditions are based on the notion that profits trump the BEST INTERESTS of people, particularly those with the ability to exploit others for personal gain.

THE BALL DOCTRINE points out the absolute need to *reign-in* the money powers that have created so much harm to so many people throughout World History. This was President Kennedy's vision:

'He believed the family *reigned supreme* as the basic social unit of every nation'.

Speech after speech, the affirmations of America's global supremacy over those nation's who created harm to the national security of the United States and its foreign policy directives were met head on by the Kennedy administration. Kennedy was a man of *destiny* and his policies created serious challenges for the establishment.

To that end, I have attempted to show what is lacking in the economic health of the nation. Central banks cause harm in the modern world because their policies are corrupted from within by policies created in 1910 and beyond starting at *Jekyl Island, Georgia.*

What is needed now is an act that corrects and cancels the harm that began over 100 years ago.

'THE BALL ACT' makes it possible. Conceived in *Liberty*, the act affirms the treason of Woodrow Wilson signing the

Federal Reserve Act on December 23, 1913 while Congress was out of session during Christmas.

A progressive, he violated his Oath of Office as President allowing enemies of The People to exploit the Constitution! As long as Central Banks could charge the federal government interest on non-backed money, the corrupt establishment allowed it to pass. President Kennedy knew the Constitutional Powers of Separation of the three branches of government and that in effect it was the United States Treasury should be in control of America's *monetary and currency policy.*

This violation of America's sovereignty showed Kennedy what previous Presidents also knew: 'The issuing of money was to come through Congress; not a Central Bank!

In other words, the nation's business was to stay with the nation; affirmed by previous generations and their administrations. Third party Central Banks is what Andrew Jackson shut down The Bank Of The United States during his presidency in 1833 & paid off the national debt with funds from the federal treasury backed by gold and silver bullion.

The founders had warned the nation that monetary policy could be circumvented; the nation threatened by policy violating the sovereignty of the United States causing the loss of all that had been fought and died.

With the signing of Executive Order 11110, President Kennedy effectively shut down the Federal Reserve System and they were alarmed; especially the families who benefit & support it. America's sovereignty

65

was reaffirmed and the national debt was in check. The nation was on its way to policies that would lead to greatness amongst the World's nations affirming free-enterprise Capitalism superior to Marxist-Socialist Communism in the struggle of ideas for World dominance.

The result of this act will be to return American sovereignty back to itself with a new tax system eliminating the need for its Citizens to pay interest on debt. A balance budget insures the government stays within its means to pay for what it spends. Gold & Silver returns to back government issued Tender regulated by the States as to moneys Collected from the Fair Tax on spending.

Other debt to Trust funds & Foreign Countries paid back to refund our debt.

THE BALL DOCTRINE!

Creating Peace and Prosperity
In Every Nation

by **Dennis Andrew Ball**

2020 American Party Presidential Candidate
**Author of "AMERICA 2000:
Foundations For Generations!"**
Dedicated to the memory of
President John Fitzgerald Kennedy

10. THE FED, IMF & WB

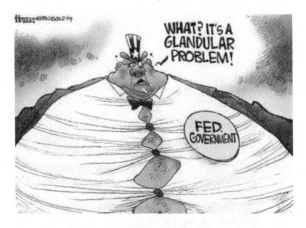

CAPITALISM makes on the nation and

the world, The People will be vilified. Years of abuse by an intrusive and corrupt system of swindle and scandal will finally be gone never to return.

The Federal Reserve System has its Tentacles in the International Monetary Fund (IMF) and the World Bank (WB).

Every nation is vulnerable to the Central Bank policy of *fiat capital* like Problems it creates in Greece & Venezuela.

The Bankers have created a fail proof System of banking that works for them at expense of their depositors. By weakening the dollar through dumping dollars into the market, prices rise because it takes more of it to pay for essential goods and services in relationship to the nation's Gross National Product (GNP). President Kennedy was all

69

over it and knew that it could bankrupt the country; something he wanted to prevent!

I believe Robert Kennedy had he become President would have continued the policies his older brother created.

Both Kennedy brothers knew that War & Money corrupt a country. Both were against the exploitation of both. That is what the bankers wanted tied to The Federal Reserve System. From it, it can be conjectured that David Rockefeller and his Tri-lateral Commission & Council of Foreign Relations have directly benefited from the power the bankers have created by this debt creating system of *fiat capital.*

11. THE GREEN NEW DEAL

It is prophesied by members of the DNC that the earth as we know it will be gone in 12 years. How that number is arrived is not known other than fake science selling people on their ignorance.

I admit environmental issues do exist but not at the expense of *real science.* I do not believe the prophets of doom of the planet have sold their arguments correctly nor do I believe we are doomed unless we transition to a Green Economy. Propaganda is easy to create by media moguls, executives & spin crafters.

Speaker of the House of Representatives in a video captured on youtube.com shared how to create a *hegel dialectic thesis, anti-thesis resolved by a synthesis.*

What this amounts to was her treatment of causing "fake news" to confuse People of her cunning and deceptive behavior causing us *harm & injury by DISTRUST!*

This is not how a leader of the Congress should ever act before her constituents or nation.

So it follows that those proponents of her enterprise have followed her lead by proposing the nation change from a fossil fuel carbon based economy to a non-fossil fueled green economy. But what does that mean?

The technology some say is here while others indicate years away from scientific achievement. The truth lies somewhere in the middle without the added stress of creating a World unable to affirm its goals.

Climate Change has been compared to Global Warming compared to excessive CO2 emissions polluting the environment in cities comprised of automobiles, trucks, heavy machinery and airport emissions.

Truth be told, the heating of the planet may be attributed to neither but a cyclical orbit of chemicals and emissions emanating from the planet itself.

The term Global Cooling is coined from temperatures exceeding 32 degrees Celsius at a rate of 10 degrees Fahrenheit. Despite clear evidence the planet is cooling, Climate Change is being touted the gloom & doom for future generations.

This author rejects this hypothesis as Propaganda by the Hegel Dialectic. The future looks bright for The People as all of us participate in preserving and protecting the environment from harmful practices of drilling and fracking.

Earth has at her core, a solid mass with hundreds of miles of surface rock leading to a hollow earth. Science does not support all of the Green House gases coming from fossil fuel emissions but emitting from nature and the planet itself.

Volcanic & Seismic activity from the earth's core shows core samples affirming different periods of change within nature's economy of planet earth. Samples taken at the poles also confirm this hypothesis.

Global Warming maybe *Global Cooling* upon which the Hegel Dialectic is mistaken for the Marxist Dialectic. The media makes the case appeals to emotions of the public "feel good" moment to cause them injury.

How? By seizing power when they are least expecting it. This is always the Modus Operandi of tyrants.

12. A NEW WAY!

AGENDA 21 is a plan for Global Governance contrary to the wishes of the Global community.

With all the forces of evil that show us their real intentions for World Domination, can we allow such a people to destroy our children and generations to come? NO!

As God is our witness to the TRUTH of Isms that cause injury and damage, let us trudge forward introducing our planet to the BEST INTERSTS of the FAMILY as God's Model for humanity and her children.

Let us decide the children are worth our investment into their lives by whatever we can do to improve them. It is our duty as citizens' of these United States to govern for their benefit and ours. "Think 1st What

Our Country Has Become, Act & Do What Must Be Done!"

Economic security is equivalent to strong Families making a "Living Wage" Skilled Labor education apprenticeships & journey men.

The People have spoken. Private property, transportation, technical advances belong to us. Managing this planet to benefit a Global Elite is contrary to attitudes & acts that benefit all our people. This is our challenge throughout the culture & into the future!

13. APPENDIX

Historical Debt Outstanding - Annual 1790 - 1849

The first fiscal year for the U.S. Government started Jan. 1, 1789. Congress changed the beginning of the fiscal year from Jan. 1 to Jul. 1 in 1842, and finally from Jul. 1 to Oct. 1 in 1977 where it remains today.

Date	Dollar Amount
07/01/1849	63,061,858.69
07/01/1848	47,044,862.23
07/01/1847	38,826,534.77
07/01/1846	15,550,202.97
07/01/1845	15,925,303.01
07/01/1844	23,461,652.50
07/01/1843	32,742,922.00
01/01/1843	20,201,226.27
01/01/1842	13,594,480.73
01/01/1841	5,250,875.54
01/01/1840	3,573,343.82
01/01/1839	10,434,221.14
01/01/1838	3,308,124.07
01/01/1837	336,957.83
01/01/1836	37,513.05

01/01/1835	33,733.05
01/01/1834	4,760,082.08
01/01/1833	7,001,698.83
01/01/1832	24,322,235.18
01/01/1831	39,123,191.68
01/01/1830	48,565,406.50
01/01/1829	58,421,413.67
01/01/1828	67,475,043.87
01/01/1827	73,987,357.20
01/01/1826	81,054,059.99
01/01/1825	83,788,432.71
01/01/1824	90,269,777.77
01/01/1823	90,875,877.28
01/01/1822	93,546,676.98
01/01/1821	89,987,427.66
01/01/1820	91,015,566.15
01/01/1819	95,529,648.28
01/01/1818	103,466,633.83
01/01/1817	123,491,965.16
01/01/1816	127,334,933.74
01/01/1815	99,833,660.15
01/01/1814	81,487,846.24
01/01/1813	55,962,827.57
01/01/1812	45,209,737.90

01/01/1811	48,005,587.76
01/01/1810	53,173,217.52
01/01/1809	57,023,192.09
01/01/1808	65,196,317.97
01/01/1807	69,218,398.64
01/01/1806	75,723,270.66
01/01/1805	82,312,150.50
01/01/1804	86,427,120.88
01/01/1803	77,054,686.40
01/01/1802	80,712,632.25
01/01/1801	83,038,050.80
01/01/1800	82,976,294.35
01/01/1799	78,408,669.77
01/01/1798	79,228,529.12
01/01/1797	82,064,479.33
01/01/1796	83,762,172.07
01/01/1795	80,747,587.39
01/01/1794	78,427,404.77
01/01/1793	80,358,634.04
01/01/1792	77,227,924.66
01/01/1791	75,463,476.52
01/01/1790	71,060,508.50

President Kennedy, The Fed And Executive Order 11110

From APFN

By Cedric X

11-20-3

Executive Order 1110 gave the US the ability to create its own money backed by silver. ...

http://www.john-f-kennedy.net/executiveorder11110.htm

On June 4, 1963, a little known attempt was made to strip the Federal Reserve Bank of its power to loan money to the government at interest. On that day President John F. Kennedy signed Executive Order No. 11110 that returned to the U.S. government the power to issue currency, without going through the Federal Reserve. Mr. Kennedy's order gave the Treasury the power "to issue silver certificates against any silver bullion, silver, or standard silver dollars in the Treasury." This meant that for every ounce of silver in the U.S. Treasury's vault, the government could introduce new money into circulation. In all, Kennedy brought nearly $4.3 billion in U.S. notes into circulation. The ramifications of this bill are enormous.

81

With the stroke of a pen, Mr. Kennedy was on his way to putting the Federal Reserve Bank of New York out of business. If enough of these silver certificates were to come into circulation they would have eliminated the demand for Federal Reserve notes. This is because the silver certificates are backed by silver and the Federal Reserve notes are not backed by anything. Executive Order 11110 could have prevented the national debt from reaching its current level, because it would have given the government the ability to repay its debt without going to the Federal Reserve and being charged interest in order to create the new money. Executive Order 11110 gave the U.S. the ability to create its own money backed by silver.

After Mr. Kennedy was assassinated just five months later, no more silver certificates were issued. The Final Call has learned that the Executive Order was never repealed by any U.S. President through an Executive Order and is still valid. Why then has no president utilized it? Virtually all of the nearly $6 trillion in debt has been created since 1963, and if a U.S. president had utilized Executive Order 11110 the debt would be nowhere near the current level. Perhaps the assassination of JFK was a warning to future presidents who would think to eliminate the U.S. debt by eliminating the Federal Reserve's control over the creation of money. Mr. Kennedy challenged the government of money by challenging

82

the two most successful vehicles that have ever been used to drive up debt - war and the creation of money by a privately-owned central bank. His efforts to have all troops out of Vietnam by 1965 and Executive Order 11110 would have severely cut into the profits and control of the New York banking establishment. As America's debt reaches unbearable levels and a conflict emerges in Bosnia that will further increase America's debt, one is force to ask, will President Clinton have the courage to consider utilizing Executive Order 11110 and, if so, is he willing to pay the ultimate price for doing so?

Executive Order 11110 AMENDMENT OF EXECUTIVE ORDER NO. 10289

AS AMENDED, RELATING TO THE PERFORMANCE OF CERTAIN FUNCTIONS AFFECTING THE DEPARTMENT OF THE TREASURY

By virtue of the authority vested in me by section 301 of title 3 of the United States Code, it is ordered as follows:

Section 1. Executive Order No. 10289 of September 19, 1951, as amended, is hereby further amended-

By adding at the end of paragraph 1 thereof the following subparagraph (j):

(j) The authority vested in the President by paragraph (b) of section 43 of the Act of May 12,1933, as amended (31 U.S.C.821(b)), to issue silver certificates against any silver bullion, silver, or standard silver dollars in the Treasury not then held for redemption of any outstanding silver certificates, to prescribe the denomination of such silver certificates, and to coin standard silver dollars and subsidiary silver currency for their redemption

and --

By revoking subparagraphs (b) and (c) of paragraph 2 thereof.

Sec. 2. The amendments made by this Order shall not affect any act done, or any right accruing or accrued or any suit or proceeding had or commenced in any civil or criminal cause prior to the date of this Order but all such liabilities shall continue and may be enforced as if said amendments had not been made.

John F. Kennedy The White House, June 4, 1963.

Of course, the fact that both JFK and Lincoln met the the same end is a mere coincidence.

Abraham Lincoln's Monetary Policy, 1865 (Page 91 of Senate document 23.)

Money is the creature of law and the creation of the original issue of money should be maintained as the exclusive monopoly of national Government.

Money possesses no value to the State other than that given to it by circulation.

Capital has its proper place and is entitled to every protection. The wages of men should be recognized in the structure of and in the social order as more important than the wages of money.

No duty is more imperative for the Government than the duty it owes the People to furnish them with a sound and uniform currency, and of regulating the circulation of the medium of exchange so that labor will be protected from a vicious currency, and commerce will be facilitated by cheap and safe exchanges.

The available supply of Gold and Silver being wholly inadequate to permit the issuance of coins of intrinsic value or paper currency convertible into coin in the volume required to serve the needs of the People, some other basis for the issue of currency must be developed, and some means other than that of convertibility into coin must be developed to prevent undue fluctuation in the value of paper currency or any other substitute for money of intrinsic value that may come into use.

The monetary needs of increasing numbers of People advancing towards higher standards of living can and should be met by the Government. Such needs can be served by the issue of National Currency and Credit through the operation of a National Banking system .The circulation of a medium of exchange issued and backed by the Government can be properly regulated and redundancy of issue avoided by withdrawing from circulation such amounts as may be necessary by Taxation, Redeposit, and otherwise. Government has the power to regulate the currency and credit of the Nation.

Government should stand behind its currency and credit and the Bank deposits of the Nation. No individual should suffer a loss of money through depreciation or inflated currency or Bank bankruptcy.

Government possessing the power to create and issue currency and creditas money and enjoying the right to withdraw both currency and credit from circulation by Taxation and otherwise need not and should not borrow capital at interest as a means of financing Governmental work and public enterprise. The Government should create, issue, and circulate all the currency and credit needed to satisfy the spending power of the Government and the buying power of the consumers. The privilege of creating and issuing money is not only the supreme prerogative of Government, but it is the Governments greatest creative opportunity.

By the adoption of these principles the long felt want for a uniform medium will be satisfied. The taxpayers will be saved immense sums of interest, discounts, and exchanges. The financing of all public enterprise, the maintenance of stable Government and ordered progress, and the conduct of the Treasury will become matters of practical administration. The people can and will be furnished with a currency as safe as their own Government. Money will cease to be master and become the servant of humanity. Democracy will rise superior to the money power.

Some information on the Federal Reserve The Federal Reserve, a Private Corporation One of the most common concerns among people who engage in any effort to reduce their taxes is, "Will keeping my money hurt the government's ability to pay it's bills?"

As explained in the first article in this series, the modern withholding tax does not, and wasn't designed to, pay for government services. What it does do, is pay for the privately-owned Federal Reserve System.

Black's Law Dictionary defines the "Federal Reserve System" as, "Network of twelve central banks to which most national banks belong and to which state chartered banks may belong. Membership rules require investment of stock and minimum reserves."

Privately-owned banks own the stock of the Fed. This was explained in more detail in the case of Lewis v. United States, Federal Reporter, 2nd Series, Vol. 680, Pages 1239, 1241 (1982), where the court said:

Each Federal Reserve Bank is a separate corporation owned by commercial banks in its region. The stock-holding commercial banks elect two thirds of each Bank's nine member board of directors.

Similarly, the Federal Reserve Banks, though heavily regulated, are locally controlled by their member banks. Taking another look at Black's Law Dictionary, we find that these privately owned banks actually issue money:

Federal Reserve Act. Law which created Federal
Reserve banks which act as agents in maintaining
money reserves, issuing money in the form of bank
notes, lending money to banks, and supervising
banks. Administered by Federal Reserve Board
(q.v.).

The FED banks, which are privately owned, actually
issue, that is, create, the money we use. In 1964 the
House Committee on Banking and Currency,
Subcommittee on Domestic Finance, at the second
session of the 88th Congress, put out a study entitled
Money Facts which contains a good description of
what the FED is:

The Federal Reserve is a total money-making
machine. It can issue money or checks. And it never
has a problem of making its checks good because it
can obtain the $5 and $10 bills necessary to cover its
check simply by asking the Treasury Department's
Bureau of Engraving to print them.

As we all know, anyone who has a lot of money has a
lot of power. Now imagine a group of people who
have the power to create money. Imagine the power
these people would have. This is what the Fed is.

No man did more to expose the power of the Fed than Louis T. McFadden, who was the Chairman of the House Banking Committee back in the 1930s. Constantly pointing out that monetary issues shouldn't be partisan, he criticized both the Herbert Hoover and Franklin Roosevelt administrations. In describing the Fed, he remarked in the Congressional Record, House pages 1295 and 1296 on June 10, 1932, that:

Mr. Chairman, we have in this country one of the most corrupt institutions the world has ever known. I refer to the Federal Reserve Board and the Federal reserve banks. The Federal Reserve Board, a Government Board, has cheated the Government of the United States and he people of the United States out of enough money to pay the national debt. The depredations and the iniquities of the Federal Reserve Board and the Federal reserve banks acting together have cost this country enough money to pay the national debt several times over. This evil institution has impoverished and ruined the people of the United States; has bankrupted itself, and has practically bankrupted our Government. It has done this through the maladministration of that law by which the Federal Reserve Board, and through the corrupt practices of the moneyed vultures who control it.

Some people think the Federal reserve banks are United States Government institutions. They are not Government institutions. They are private credit monopolies which prey upon the people of the United States for the benefit of themselves and their foreign customers; foreign and domestic speculators and swindlers; and rich and predatory money lenders. In that dark crew of financial pirates there are those who would cut a man's throat to get a dollar out of his pocket; there are those who send money into States to buy votes to control our legislation; and there are those who maintain an international propaganda for the purpose of deceiving us and of wheedling us into the granting of new concessions which will permit them to cover up their past misdeeds and set again in motion their gigantic train of crime. Those 12 private credit monopolies were deceitfully and disloyally foisted upon this country by bankers who came here from Europe and who repaid us for our hospitality by undermining our American institutions.

The Fed basically works like this: The government granted its power to create money to the Fed banks. They create money, then loan it back to the government charging interest. The government levies income taxes to pay the interest on the debt. On this point, it's interesting to note that the Federal Reserve act and the sixteenth amendment, which gave congress the power to collect income taxes, were both passed in 1913. The incredible power of the Fed over the economy is universally admitted. Some people, especially in the banking and academic communities, even support it. On the other hand, there are those, both in the past and in the present, that speak out against it. One of these men was

President John F. Kennedy. His efforts were detailed in Jim Marrs' 1990 book, Crossfire:

Another overlooked aspect of Kennedy's attempt to reform American society involves money. Kennedy apparently reasoned that by returning to the constitution, which states that only Congress shall coin and regulate money, the soaring national debt could be reduced by not paying interest to the bankers of the Federal Reserve System, who print paper money then loan it to the government at interest. He moved in this area on June 4, 1963, by signing Executive Order 11,110 which called for the issuance of $4,292,893,815 in United States Notes through the U.S. Treasury rather than the traditional Federal Reserve System. That same day, Kennedy signed a bill changing the backing of one and two dollar bills from silver to gold, adding strength to the weakened U.S. currency.

Kennedy's comptroller of the currency, James J. Saxon, had been at odds with the powerful Federal Reserve Board for some time, encouraging broader investment and lending powers for banks that were not part of the Federal Reserve system. Saxon also had decided that non-Reserve banks could underwrite state and local general obligation bonds, again weakening the dominant Federal Reserve banks.

A number of "Kennedy bills" were indeed issued - the author has a five dollar bill in his possession with the heading "United States Note" - but were quickly withdrawn after Kennedy's death. According to information from the Library of the Comptroller of the Currency, Executive Order 11,110 remains in effect today, although successive administrations beginning with that of President Lyndon Johnson apparently have simply ignored it and instead returned to the practice of paying interest on Federal Reserve notes. Today we continue to use Federal Reserve Notes, and the deficit is at an all-time high.

The point being made is that the IRS taxes you pay aren't used for government services. It won't hurt you, or the nation, to legally reduce or eliminate your tax liability.

From The Final Call, Vol15, No.6, on January 17, 1996 (USA)

<http://www.apfn.org/apfn/eo11110.pdf>http://www.apfn.org/apfn/eo11110.pdf

http://disc.server.com/discussion.cgi?disc=149495;article=46736;title=APFN

JFK vs. Federal Reserve

On June 4, 1963, a virtually unknown Presidential decree, Executive Order 11110, was signed by President John Fitzgerald Kennedy with the intention to strip the Federal Reserve Bank of its power to loan money to the United States Federal Government at interest. With the stroke of a pen, President Kennedy declared that the privately owned Federal Reserve Bank would soon be out of business. This matter has been exhaustively researched by the Christian Common Law Institute through the Federal Register and Library of Congress, and the Institute has conclude that President Kennedy's Executive Order has never been repealed, amended, or superceded by any subsequent Executive Order. In simple terms, it is still valid.

When John Fitzgerald Kennedy, author of Profiles in Courage, signed this Order, it returned to the federal government, specifically to the Treasury Department, the Constitutional power to create and issue currency -- money -- without going through the privately owned Federal Reserve Bank. President Kennedy's Executive Order 11110 gave the Treasury Department the explicit authority: "to issue silver certificates against any silver bullion, silver, or standard silver dollars in the Treasury" [the full text is displayed below]. This means that for every ounce of silver in the U.S. Treasury's vault, the government could introduce new money into circulation based on the silver bullion physically held therein. As a result, more than $4 billion in United States Notes were brought into circulation in $2 and $5 denominations.

Although $10 and $20 United States Notes were never circulated, they were being printed by the Treasury Department when Kennedy was assassinated.

Certainly it's obvious that President Kennedy knew that the Federal Reserve Notes being circulated as "legal currency" were contrary to the Constitution of the United States, which calls for issuance of "United States Notes" as interest-free and debt-free currency backed by silver reserves in the U.S. Treasury. Comparing a "Federal Reserve Note" issued from the private central bank of the United States (i.e., the Federal Reserve Bank a/k/a Federal Reserve System), with a "United States Note" from the U.S. Treasury (as issued by President Kennedy's Executive Order), the two almost look alike, except one says "Federal Reserve Note" on the top while the other says "United States Note". In addition, the Federal Reserve Note has a green seal and serial number while the United States Note has a red seal and serial number. Following President Kennedy's assassination on November 22, 1963, the United States Notes he had issued were immediately taken out of circulation, and Federal Reserve Notes continued to serve as the "legal currency" of the nation.

Kennedy knew that if the silver-backed United States Notes were widely circulated, they would eliminated the demand for Federal Reserve Notes. This is a simple matter of economics. USNs were backed by silver and FRNs were (still are) backed by nothing of intrinsic value. As a result of Executive Order 11110, the national debt would have prevented from reaching its current level (almost all of the $9 trillion in federal debt has been created since 1963). Executive Order 11110 also granted the U.S. Government the power to repay past debt without further borrowing from the privately owned Federal Reserve which charged both principle and interest and all new "money" it "created." Finally, Executive Order 11110 gave the U.S.A. the ability to create its own money backed by silver, again giving money real value.

Perhaps President Kennedy's assassination was a warning to future presidents not to interfere with the private Federal Reserve's control over the creation of money. For, with true courage, JFK had boldly challenged the two most successful vehicles that have ever been used to drive up debt: 1) war (i.e., the Vietnam war); and, 2) the creation of money by a privately owned central bank. His efforts to have all U.S. troops out of Vietnam by 1965 combined with Executive Order 11110 would have destroyed the profits and control of the private Federal Reserve Bank.

Executive Order 11110, the AMENDMENT of EXECUTIVE ORDER No. 10289, as amended RELATING to the PERFORMANCE of CERTAIN

FUNCTIONS AFFECTING the DEPARTMENT of the TREASURY:

By virtue of the authority vested in me by section 301 of Title 3 of the United States Code, it is ordered as follows:

SECTION 1. Executive Order No. 10289 of September 19, 1951, as amended, is hereby further amended (a) By adding at the end of paragraph 1 thereof the following subparagraph (j): "(j) The authority vested in the President by paragraph (b) of section 43 of the Act of May 12, 1933, as amended (31 U.S.C. 821 (b)), to issue silver certificates against any silver bullion, silver, or standard silver dollars in the Treasury not then held for redemption of any outstanding silver certificates, to prescribe the denominations of such silver certificates, and to coin standard silver dollars and subsidiary silver currency for their redemption," and (b) By revoking subparagraphs (b) and (c) of paragraph 2 thereof.

SECTION 2. The amendment made by this Order shall not affect any act done, or any right accruing or accrued or any suit or proceeding had or commenced in any civil or criminal cause prior to the date of this Order but all such liabilities shall continue and may be enforced as if said amendments had not been made.

JOHN F. KENNEDY

THE WHITE HOUSE,

June 4, 1963

As said, Executive Order 11110 is still valid. According to Title 3, United States Code, Section 301 dated January 26, 1998: Executive Order (EO) 10289 dated Sept. 17, 1951, 16 F.R. 9499, was as amended by:

EO 10583, dated December 18, 1954, 19 F.R. 8725;

EO 10882 dated July 18, 1960, 25 F.R. 6869;

EO 11110 dated June 4, 1963, 28 F.R. 5605;

EO 11825 dated December 31, 1974, 40 F.R. 1003;

EO 12608 dated September 9, 1987, 52 F.R. 34617

The 1974 and 1987 amendments, added after Kennedy's 1963 amendment, did not change or alter any part of Kennedy's EO 11110. A search of Clinton's 1998 and 1999 EO's and Presidential Directives has shown no reference to any alterations, suspensions, or changes to EO 11110.

The Federal Reserve Bank, a.k.a Federal Reserve System, is a Private Corporation. Black's Law Dictionary defines the "Federal Reserve System" as:

"Network of twelve central banks to which most national banks belong and to which state chartered banks may belong. Membership rules require investment of stock and minimum reserves." privately owned banks own the stock of the FED. This was explained in more detail in the case of Lewis v. United States, Federal Reporter, 2nd Series, Vol. 680, Pages 1239, 1241 (1982), where the court said: "Each Federal Reserve Bank is a separate corporation owned by commercial banks in its region. The stockholding commercial banks elect two-thirds of each Bank's nine member board of directors." In short, Federal Reserve Banks are locally controlled by their member banks.

Also, according to Black's Law Dictionary, these privately owned banks are "allowed" to issue money: "The Federal Reserve Act, created Federal Reserve banks which act as agents in maintaining money reserves, issuing money in the form of bank notes, lending money to banks, and supervising banks as administered by Federal Reserve Board (q.v.)." Thus the privately owned Federal Reserve (FED) banks are allowed to actually issue (create) the "money" we use.

In 1964, the House Committee on Banking and Currency, Subcommittee on Domestic Finance, at the second session of the 88th Congress, put out a study entitled Money Facts which contains a good description of what the FED is: "The Federal Reserve is a total moneymaking machine. It can issue money or checks. And it never has a problem of making its checks good because it can obtain the $5 and $10 bills necessary to cover its check simply by asking the Treasury Department's Bureau of Engraving to print them." Any one person or any closely knit group that has a lot of money has a lot of power. Imagine a group of people with the power to create money. Imagine the power these people would have. This is exactly what the privately owned FED is!

No man did more to expose the power of the FED than Louis T. McFadden, who was the Chairman of the House Banking Committee back in the 1930s. In describing the FED, he remarked in the Congressional Record, House pages 1295 and 1296 on June 10, 1932:

Mr. Chairman, we have in this country one of the most corrupt institutions the world has ever known. I refer to the Federal Reserve Board and the Federal reserve banks. The Federal Reserve Board, a Government Board, has cheated the Government of the United States and he people of the United States out of enough money to pay the national debt. The depredations and the iniquities of the Federal Reserve Board and the Federal reserve banks acting together have cost this country enough money to pay the national debt several times over. This evil institution has impoverished and ruined the people of the United States; has bankrupted itself, and has practically bankrupted our Government. It has done this through the maladministration of that law by which the Federal Reserve Board, and through the corrupt practices of the moneyed vultures who control it.

Some people think the Federal Reserve Banks are United States Government institutions. They are not Government institutions, departments, or agencies. They are private credit monopolies, which prey upon the people of the United States for the benefit of themselves and their foreign customers. Those 12 private credit monopolies were deceitfully placed upon this country by bankers who came here from Europe and who repaid us for our hospitality by undermining our American institutions.

The FED basically works like this: The government granted its power to create money to the FED banks. They create money, then loan it back to the government charging interest. The government levies income taxes to pay the interest on the debt. On this point, it's interesting to note that the Federal Reserve Act and the sixteenth amendment, which gave congress the power to collect income taxes, were both passed in 1913. The incredible power of the FED over the economy is universally admitted. Some people, especially in the banking and academic communities, support it. On the other hand, there are those like President John F. Kennedy, that have spoken out against it. His efforts were lauded about in Jim Marrs' 1990 book Crossfire:

Another overlooked aspect of Kennedy's attempt to reform American society involves money. Kennedy apparently reasoned that by returning to the constitution, which states that only Congress shall coin and regulate money, the soaring national debt could be reduced by not paying interest to the bankers of the Federal Reserve System, who print paper money then loan it to the government at interest. He moved in this area on June 4, 1963, by signing Executive Order 11110 which called for the issuance of $4,292,893,815 in United States Notes through the U.S. Treasury rather than the traditional Federal Reserve System. That same day, Kennedy signed a bill changing the backing of one and two dollar bills from silver to gold, adding strength to the weakened U.S. currency.

Kennedy's comptroller of the currency, James J. Saxon, had been at odds with the powerful Federal Reserve Board for some time, encouraging broader investment and lending powers for banks that were not part of the Federal Reserve system. Saxon also had decided that non-Reserve banks could underwrite general obligation bonds, again weakening the dominant Federal Reserve banks."

In a speech made to Columbia University on Nov. 12, 1963, ten days before his assassination, President John Fitzgerald Kennedy said: "The high office of the

President has been used to foment a plot to destroy the American's freedom and before I leave office, I must inform the citizen of this plight." In this matter, John Fitzgerald Kennedy appears to be the subject of his own book... a true Profile of Courage. According to the Constitution of the United States, (Article 1 Section 8), only Congress has the authority to coin Money, regulate the Value thereof, and of foreign Coin, and fix the Standard of Weights and Measures. However, since 1913 this Article has been ignored by creation and existence of the Federal Reserve Act, which has given a private owned corporation the power and authority to "create" and coin the money of United States. The Federal Reserve is comprised of 12 private credit monopolies who have been given the authority to control the supply of the "Federal Reserve Notes," interest rates and all the other monetary and banking phenomena.

The way the Federal Reserve works is this: 12 private credit monopolies "create", (print), Federal Reserve Notes that are then "lent" to the American government. This is a circular affair in that the government grants the FED power to create the money, which the FED then loans back to the government, charging interests. The government levies income taxes to pay the interest on the debt. It is interesting to note that the Federal Reserve Act and the sixteenth amendment which gave congress the power to collect income taxes, were both passed in 1913. The Federal Reserve Notes are not backed by anything of "intrinsic" value. (i.e., gold or silver).

103

On June 4, 1963, President, John Fitzgerald Kennedy signed a Presidential decree, Executive Order 11110, which stripped the Federal Reserve Banking System of its power to loan money to the United States Federal Government at interest. This decree meant that for every ounce of silver in the U.S. Treasury's vault, the U.S. government could introduce new money into circulation based on the silver bullion physically held therein. As a result, more than $4 trillion in United States Notes were brought into circulation in $2 and $5 denominations. $10 and $20 United States Notes were never circulated but were being printed by the Treasury Department when Kennedy was assassinated. Kennedy knew that if the silver backed United States Notes were widely circulated, they would have eliminated the demand for Federal Reserve Notes. By giving the U.S. Treasury the Constitutional authority to coin U.S. money once again, EO 11110 would thus prevent the national debt from rising due to "usury" that the American people are charged for "borrowing" (i.e., using) FRN's.

Kennedy knew that, if Congress coined and regulated money, as the Constitution states, the national debt would be reduced by not paying interest to the 12 credit monopolies. This in itself would have allowed the American people freedom to freely use all the money they have earned, enabling the economy to grow. Now, Executive Order 11110 is still in effect, even though no U.S. President has had the courage to follow it. As Americans, it is our duty to question the Federal Reserve System and the power that we have given it by electing presidents that lack the courage of John Fitzgerald Kennedy.

More on JFK's Executive Order 11110:
http://www.rense.com/general44/exec.htm

REPRINTED BY PERMISSION

FOUNDATION FOR TRUTH & LAW 2017

Made in the USA
Monee, IL
25 July 2020

36989638R00059